DUKE ELLINGTON
16 JAZZ CLASSICS ARRANGED BY PHILLIP KEVEREN

Cover Photo by George Rinhart/Corbis via Getty Images

— PIANO LEVEL —
EARLY INTERMEDIATE

ISBN 978-1-5400-4669-7

HAL•LEONARD®

Visit Hal Leonard Online at
www.halleonard.com

Visit Phillip at
www.phillipkeveren.com

Contact us:
Hal Leonard
7777 West Bluemound Road
Milwaukee, WI 53213
Email: info@halleonard.com

In Europe, contact:
Hal Leonard Europe Limited
42 Wigmore Street
Marylebone, London, W1U 2RN
Email: info@halleonardeurope.com

In Australia, contact:
Hal Leonard Australia Pty. Ltd.
4 Lentara Court
Cheltenham, Victoria, 3192 Australia
Email: info@halleonard.com.au

PREFACE

Duke Ellington was a master composer, pianist, and band leader. The songs he wrote, introduced, and championed are an indelible part of the tapestry of jazz history. From the ever-popular up-tempo "Take the 'A' Train," to the elegant balladry of tunes like "Sophisticated Lady," one finds a veritable treasure trove of superb songwriting craft.

I tried to keep the technical aspects of these arrangements as clean and direct as possible, for the melodies, harmonies, and rhythms of the original compositions are intrinsically ornate. The chromaticism will test your ears at times, and you'll be tempted to wonder, "is that note correct"? It's certainly possible we have made a publishing error, but it's more likely that Duke is stretching your ear a little!

It is a pleasure to present the sophisticated music of Duke Ellington for enjoyment at the piano.

Musically yours,

Phillip Keveren

BIOGRAPHY

Phillip Keveren, a multi-talented keyboard artist and composer, has composed original works in a variety of genres from piano solo to symphonic orchestra. Mr. Keveren gives frequent concerts and workshops for teachers and their students in the United States, Canada, Europe, and Asia. He holds a B.M. in composition from California State University Northridge and a M.M. in composition from the University of Southern California.

CONTENTS

CARAVAN

Words and Music by DUKE ELLINGTON,
IRVING MILLS and JUAN TIZOL
Arranged by Phillip Keveren

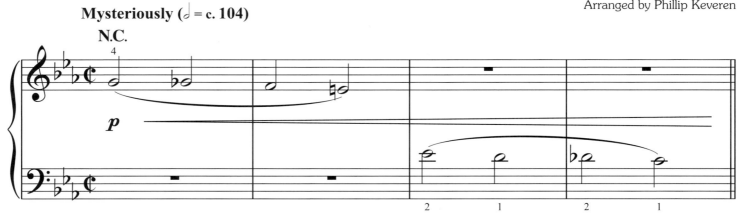

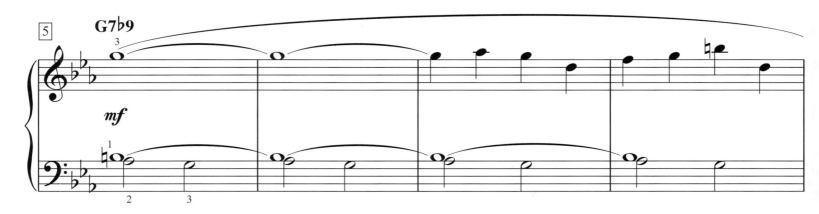

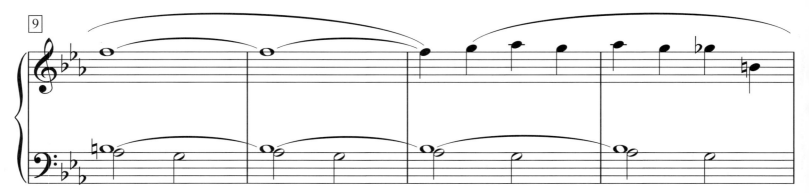

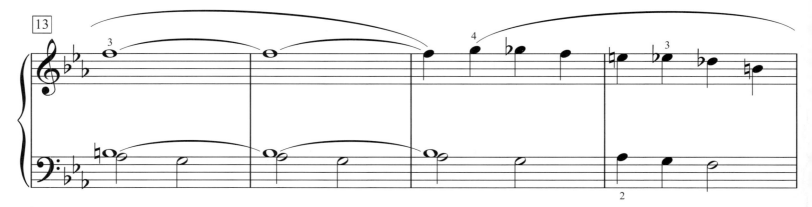

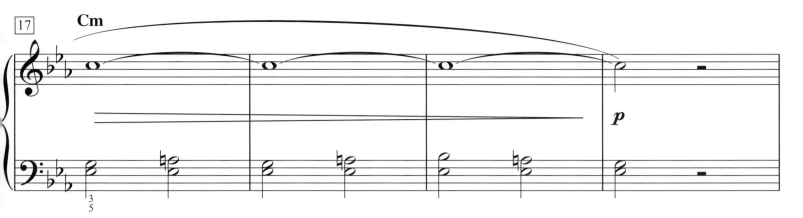

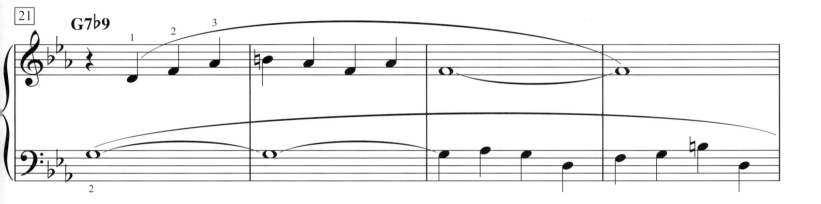

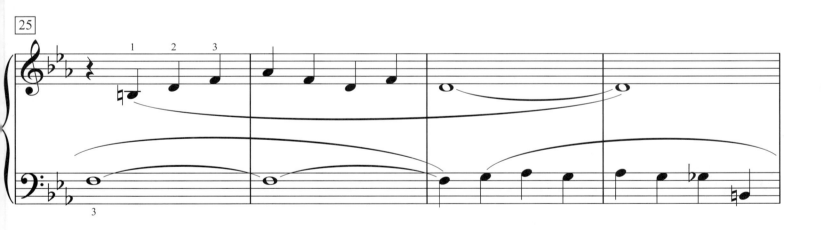

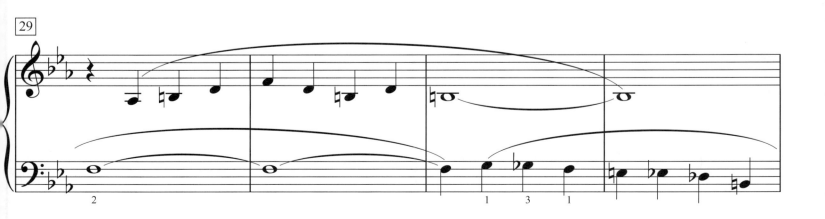

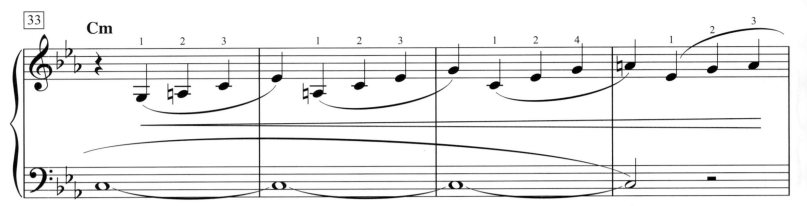

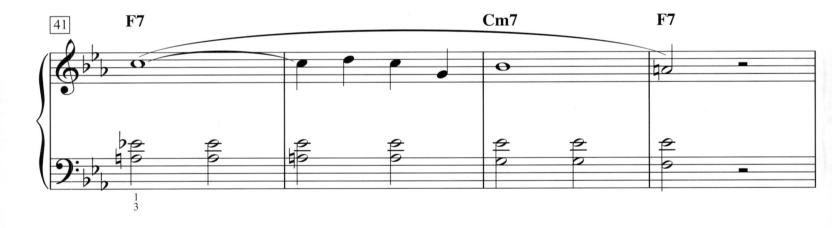

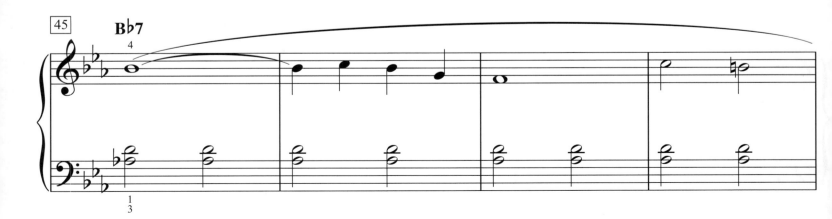

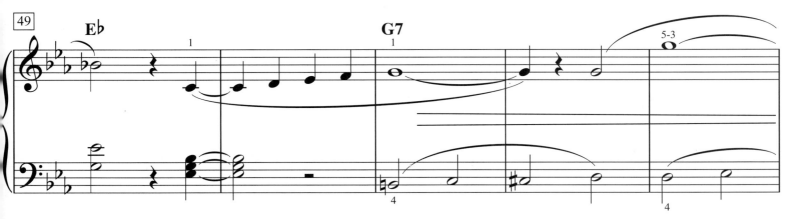

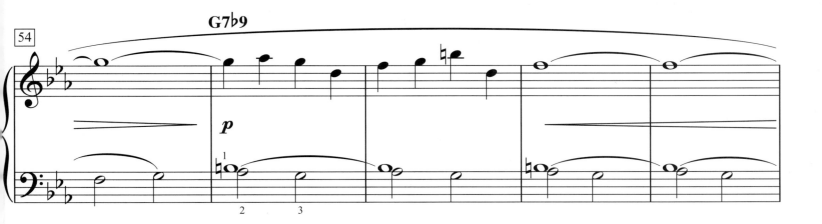

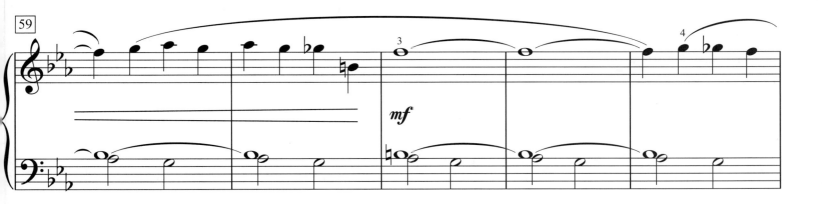

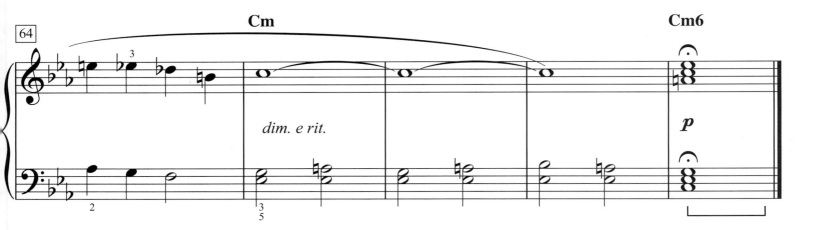

DAY DREAM

By DUKE ELLINGTON
and BILLY STRAYHORN
Arranged by Phillip Keveren

Slowly, expressively (♩ = c. 66)

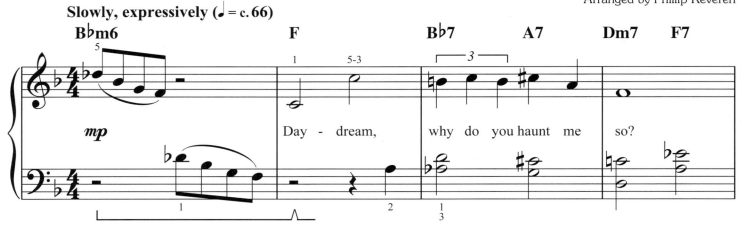

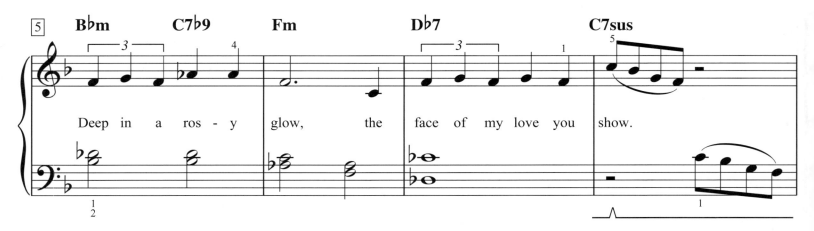

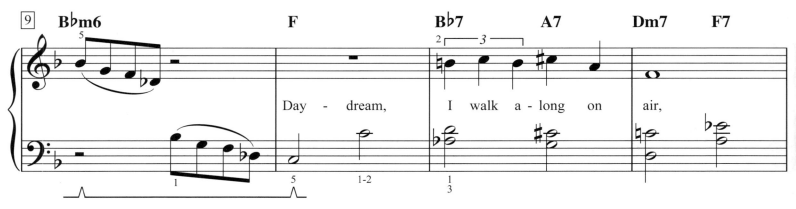

9

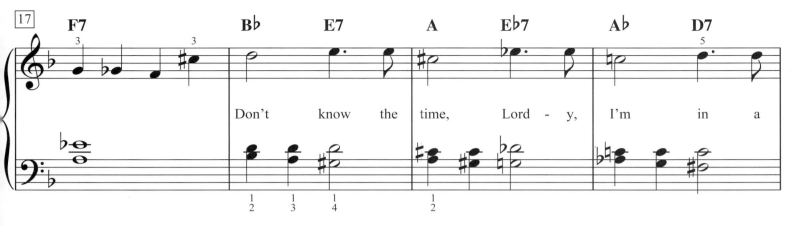

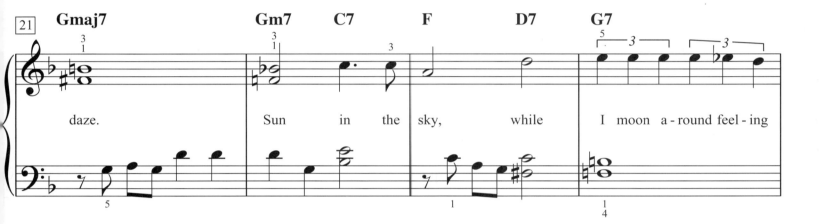

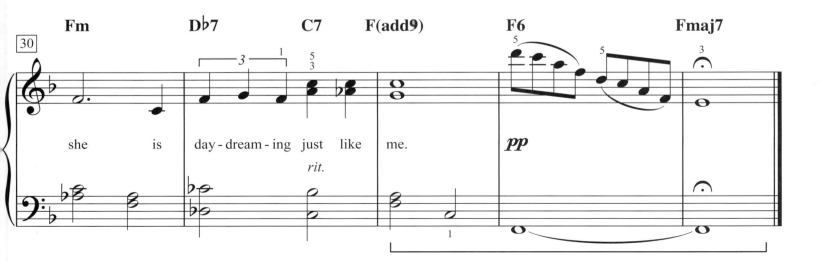

DO NOTHIN' TILL YOU HEAR FROM ME

Words and Music by DUKE ELLINGTON
and BOB RUSSELL
Arranged by Phillip Keveren

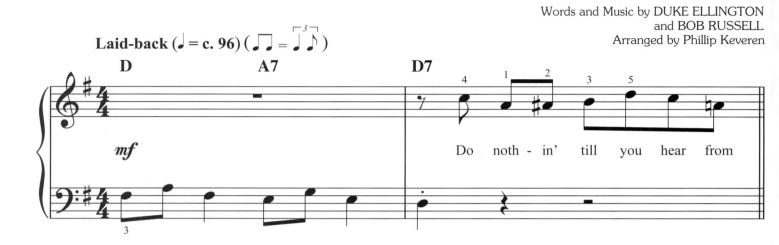

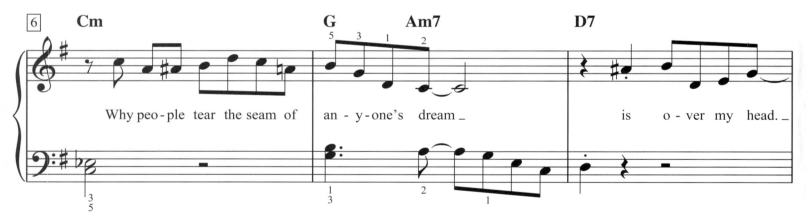

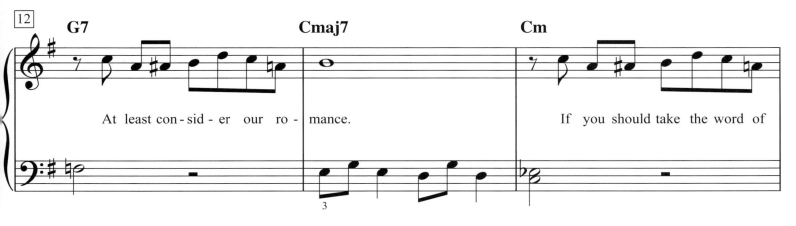

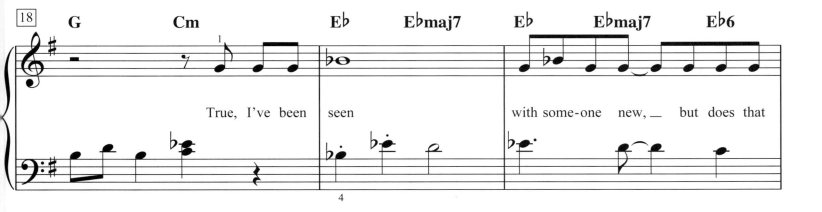

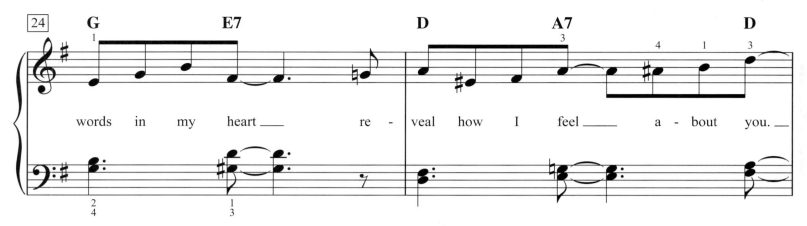

words in my heart ___ re - veal how I feel ___ a - bout you. ___

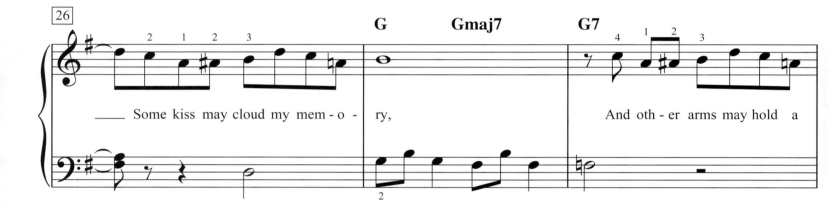

___ Some kiss may cloud my mem - o - ry, And oth - er arms may hold a

thrill, but please do noth - in' till you hear it from me, ___

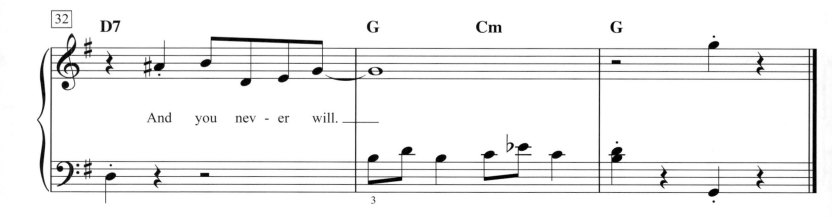

And you nev - er will. ___

DON'T GET AROUND MUCH ANYMORE

Words and Music by DUKE ELLINGTON
and BOB RUSSELL
Arranged by Phillip Keveren

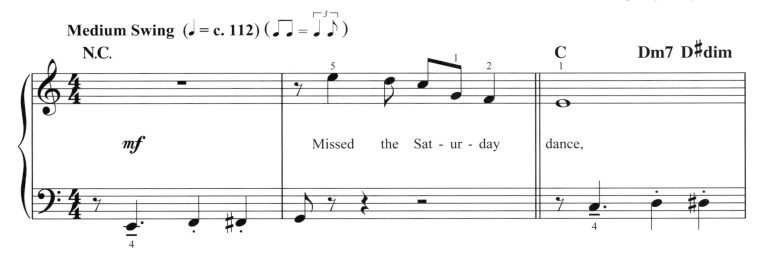

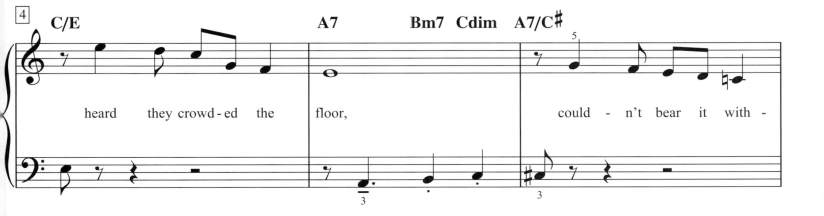

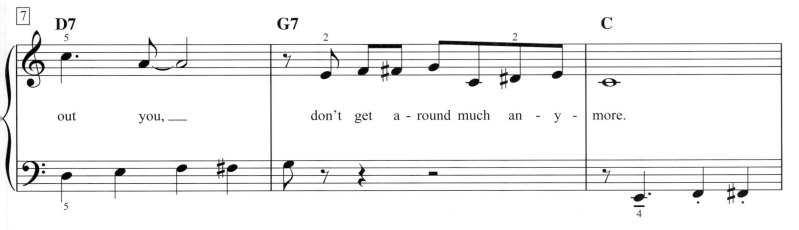

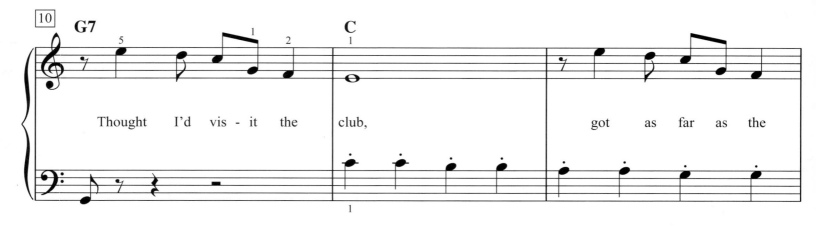

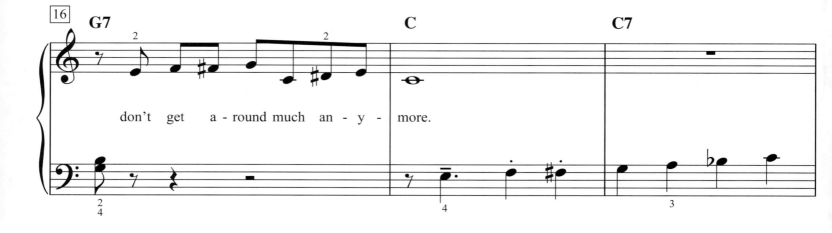

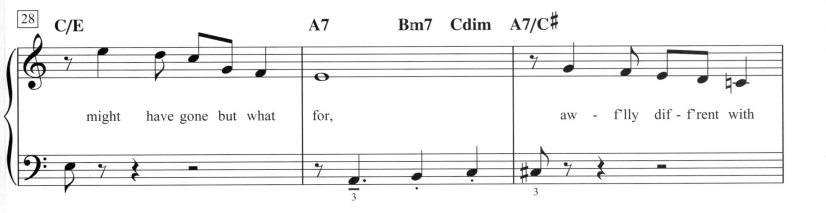

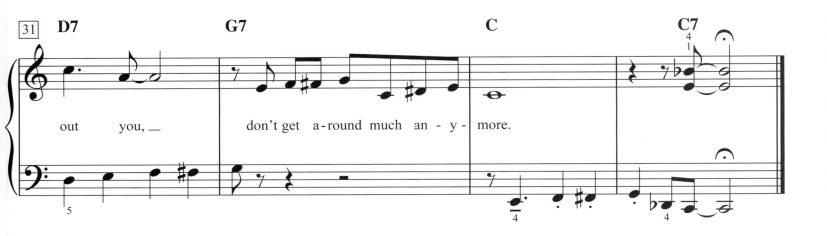

I AIN'T GOT NOTHIN' BUT THE BLUES

Words by DON GEORGE
Music by DUKE ELLINGTON
Arranged by Phillip Keveran

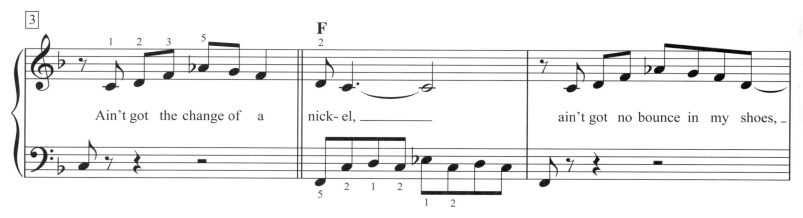

Ain't got the change of a nick-el, _____ ain't got no bounce in my shoes, _

ain't got no fan-cy to tick-le, _____

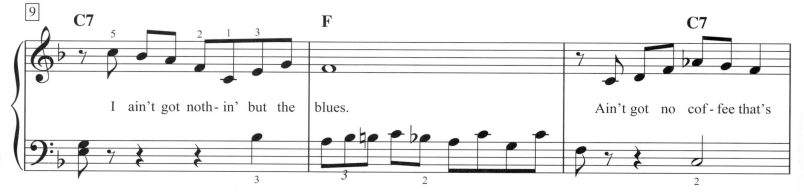

I ain't got noth-in' but the blues. Ain't got no cof-fee that's

perk - in', _____ ain't got no win-nings to lose, ____

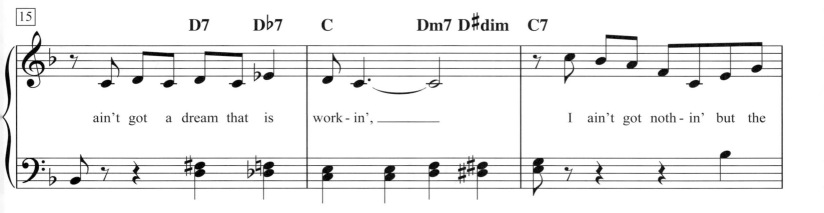

ain't got a dream that is work - in', _____ I ain't got noth - in' but the

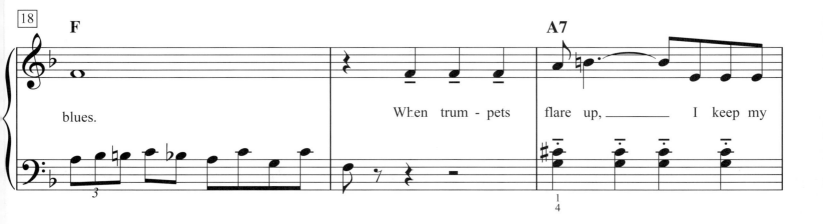

blues. When trum - pets flare up, _____ I keep my

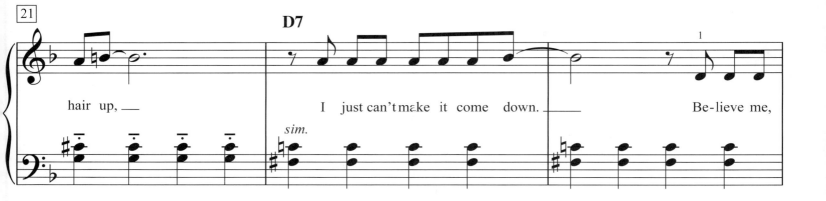

hair up, __ I just can't make it come down. _____ Be - lieve me,

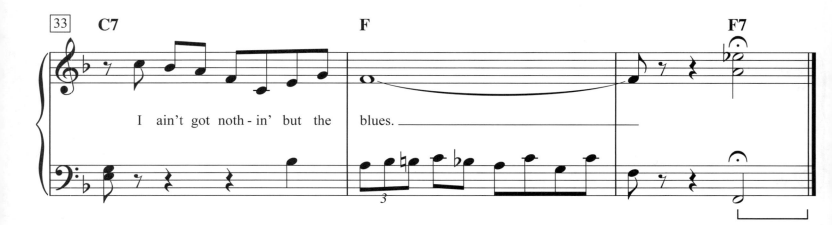

I'M BEGINNING TO SEE THE LIGHT

Words and Music by DON GEORGE, JOHNNY HODGES,
DUKE ELLINGTON and HARRY JAMES
Arranged by Phillip Keveren

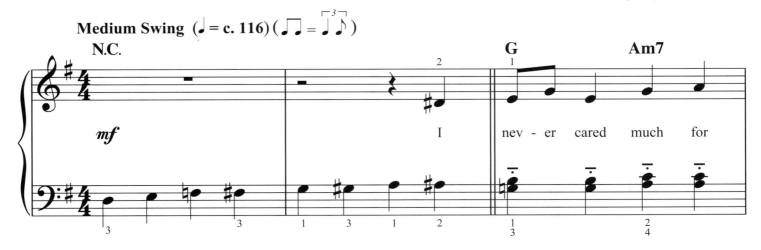

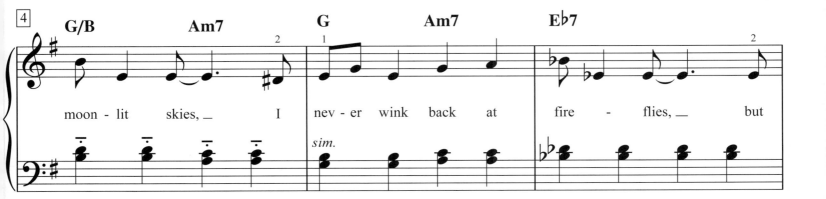

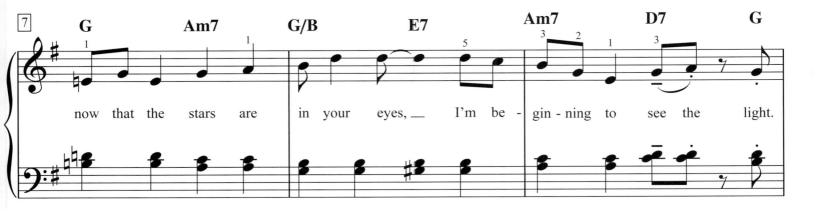

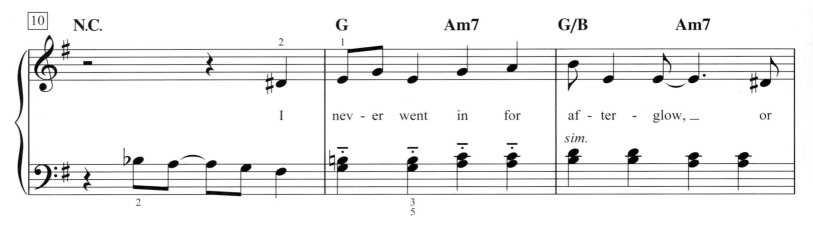

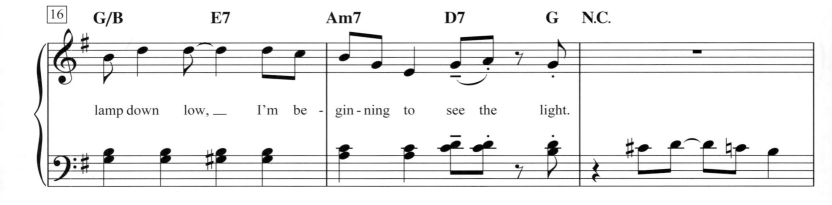

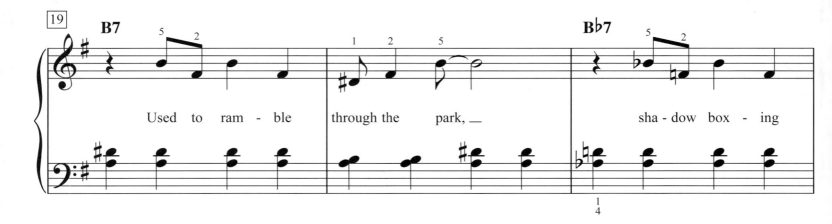

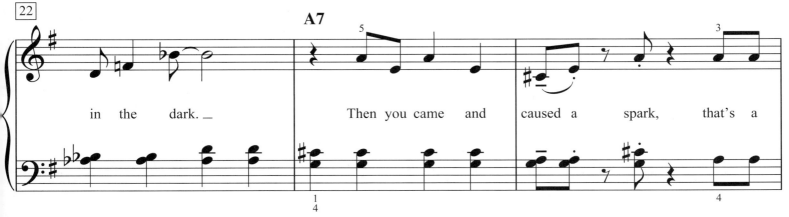

in the dark. ___ Then you came and caused a spark, that's a

four - a - larm fire ___ now. I nev - er made love by

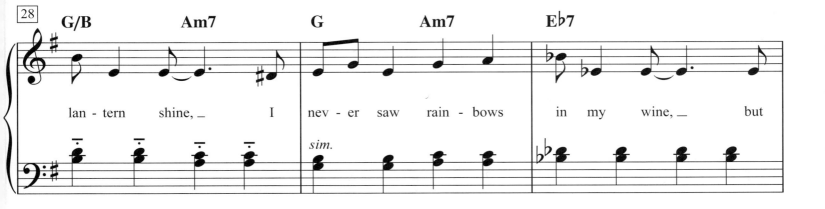

lan - tern shine, ___ I nev - er saw rain - bows in my wine, ___ but

now that your lips are burn - ing mine, ___ I'm be gin - ning to see the light.

I GOT IT BAD AND THAT AIN'T GOOD

Words by PAUL FRANCIS WEBSTER
Music by DUKE ELLINGTON
Arranged by Phillip Keveren

Melancholy Ballad (♩ = c. 88)

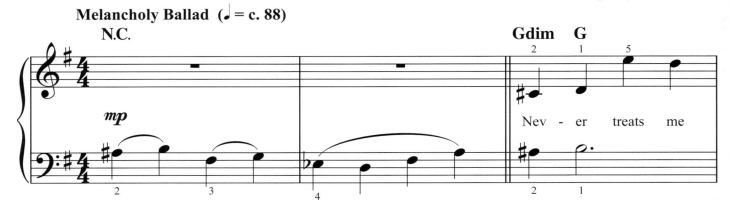

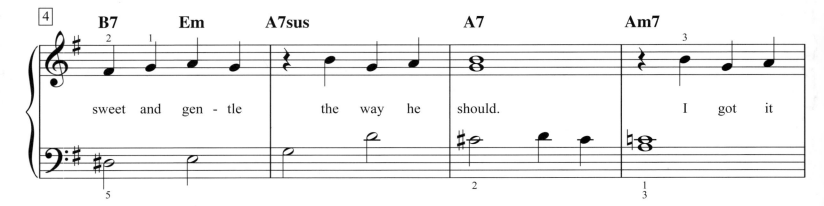

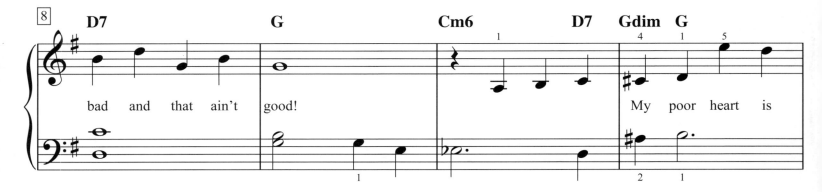

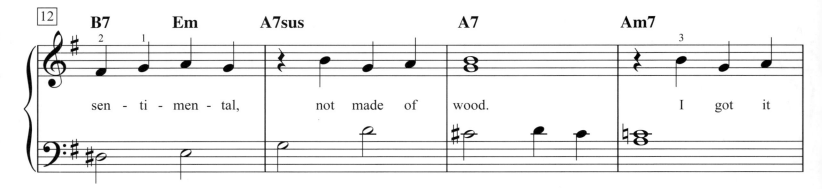

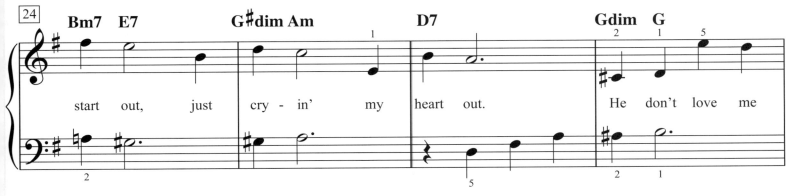

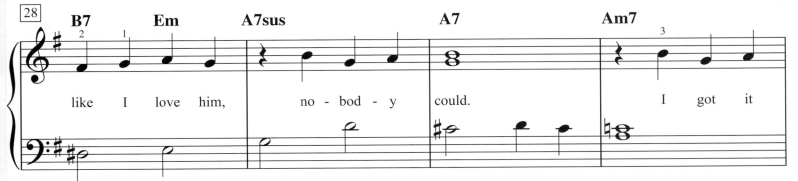

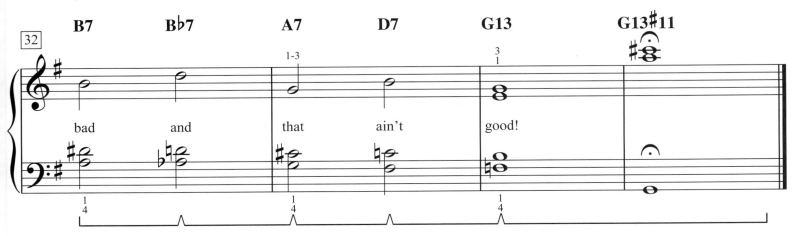

IN A SENTIMENTAL MOOD

By DUKE ELLINGTON
Arranged by Phillip Keveren

Tenderly ($\quad$ = c. 72)

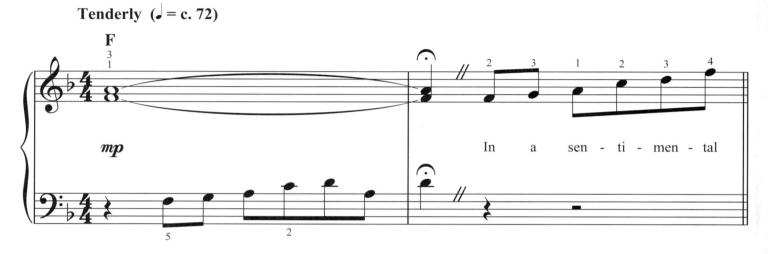

In a sen - ti - men - tal

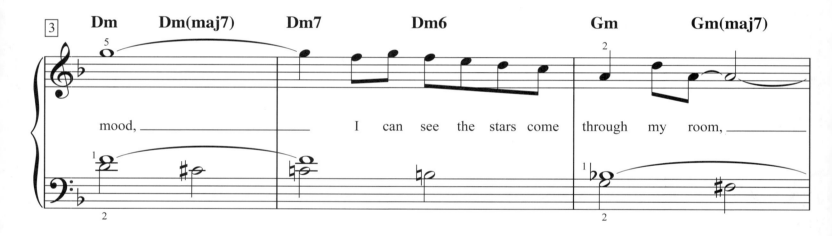

mood, _____ I can see the stars come through my room, _____

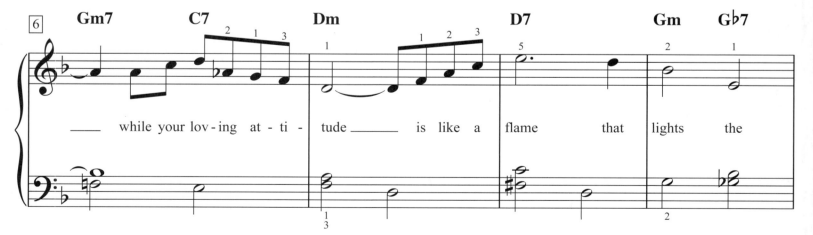

_____ while your lov-ing at-ti- tude _____ is like a flame that lights the

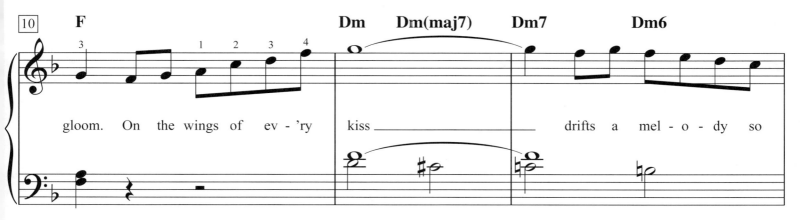

gloom. On the wings of ev - 'ry kiss ___ drifts a mel - o - dy so

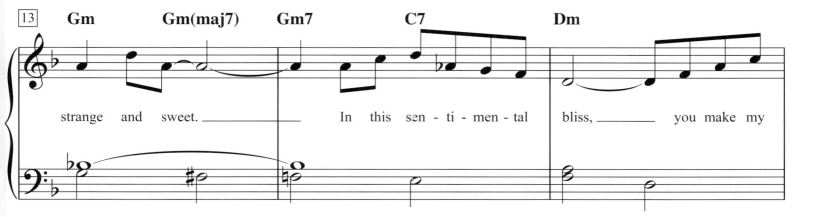

strange and sweet. ___ In this sen - ti - men - tal bliss, ___ you make my

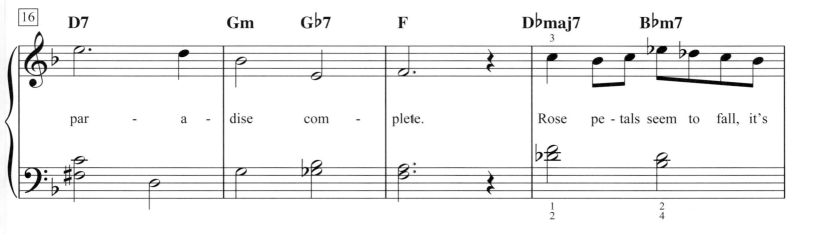

par - a - dise com - plete. Rose pe - tals seem to fall, it's

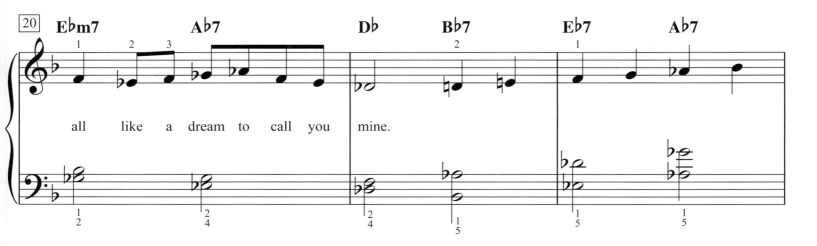

all like a dream to call you mine.

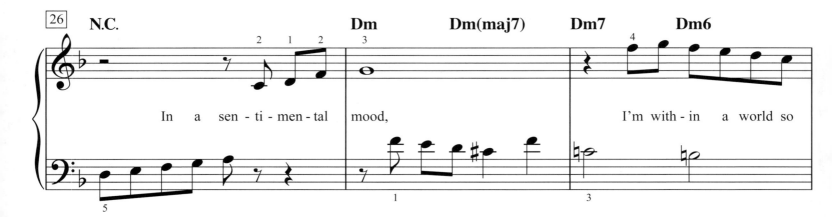

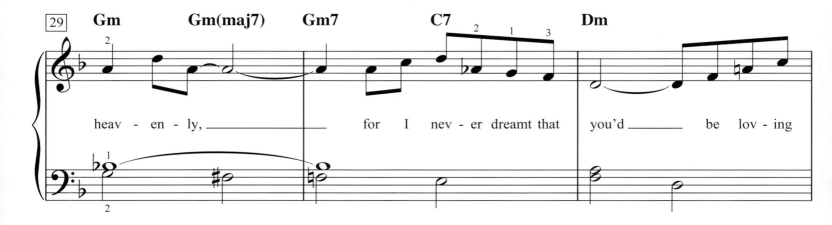

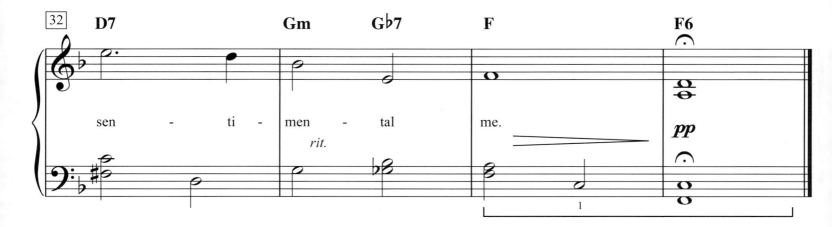

IT DON'T MEAN A THING
(If It Ain't Got That Swing)

Words and Music by DUKE ELLINGTON
and IRVING MILLS
Arranged by Phillip Keveren

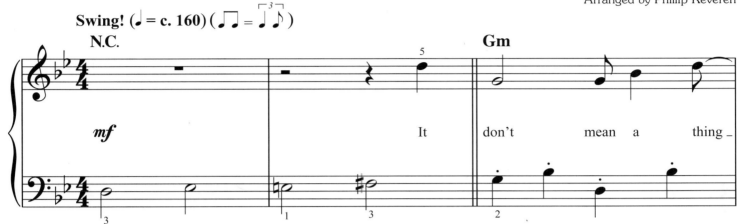

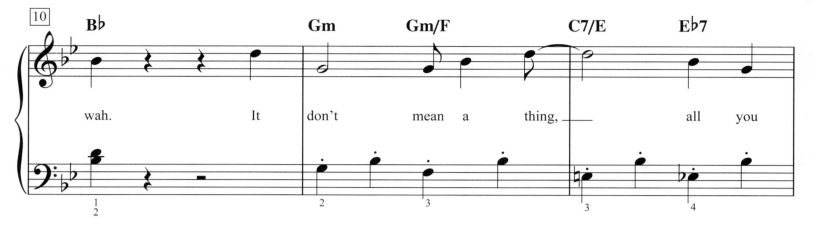

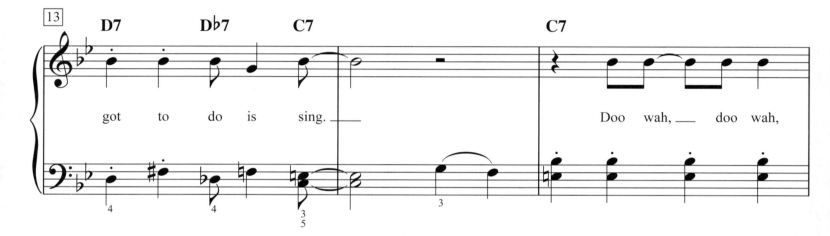

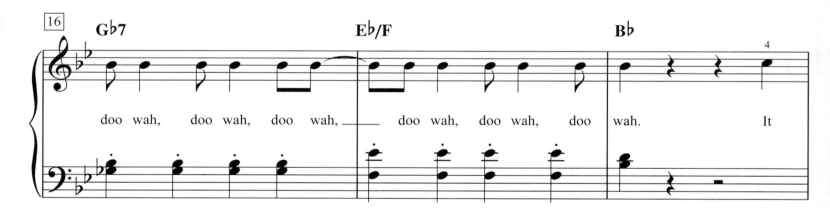

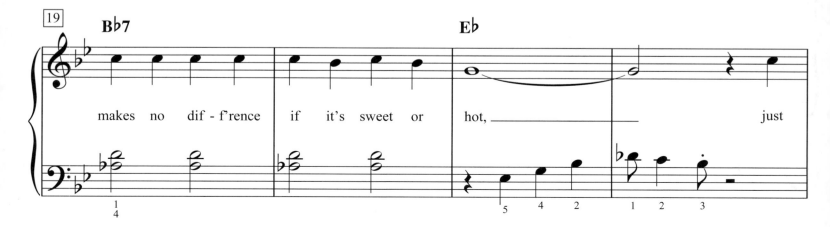

give that rhy - thm ev - 'ry - thing you got. ___

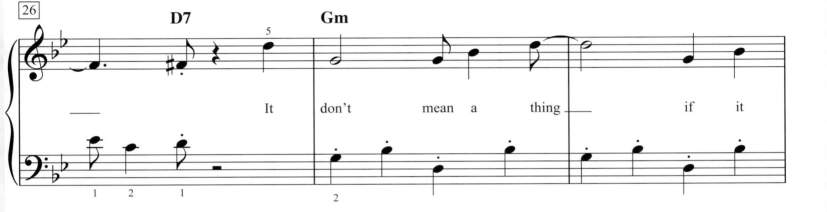

___ It don't mean a thing ___ if it

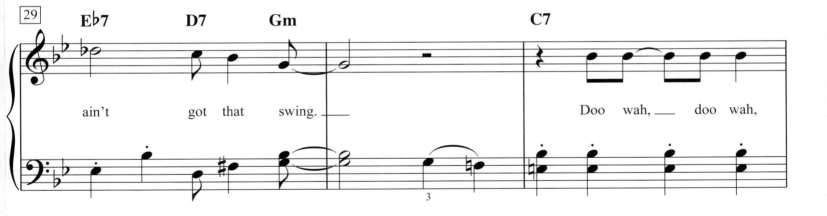

ain't got that swing. ___ Doo wah, ___ doo wah,

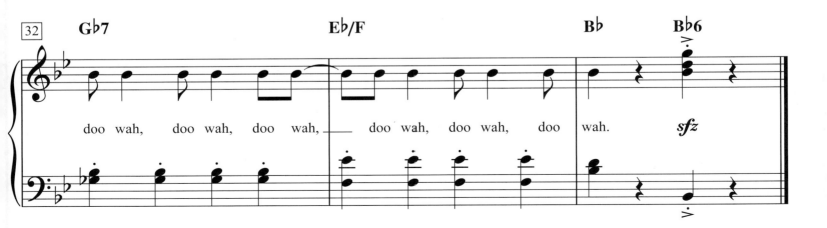

doo wah, doo wah, doo wah, ___ doo wah, doo wah, doo wah. sfz

MOOD INDIGO

Words and Music by DUKE ELLINGTON,
IRVING MILLS and ALBANY BIGARD
Arranged by Phillip Keveren

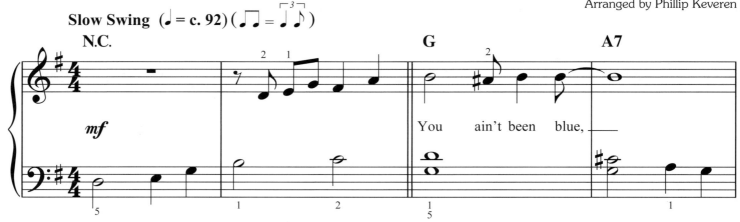

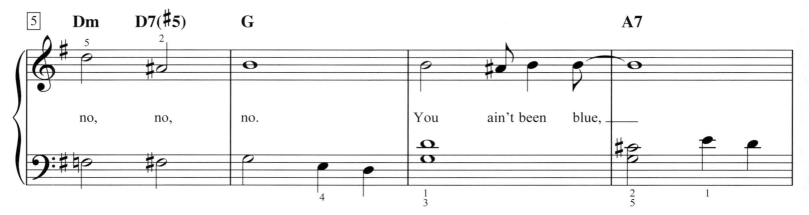

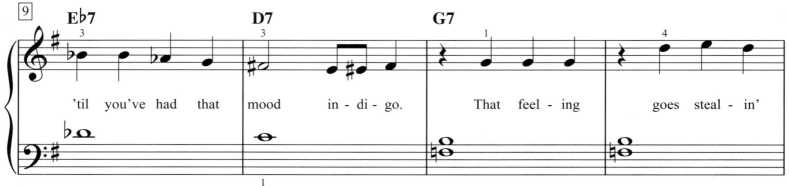

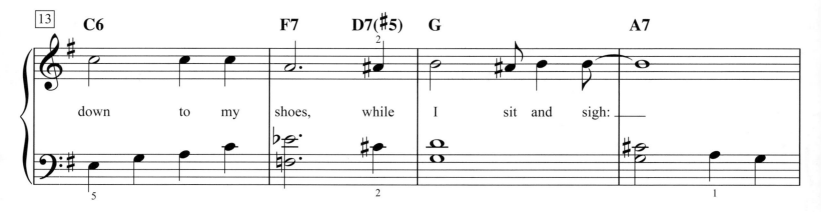

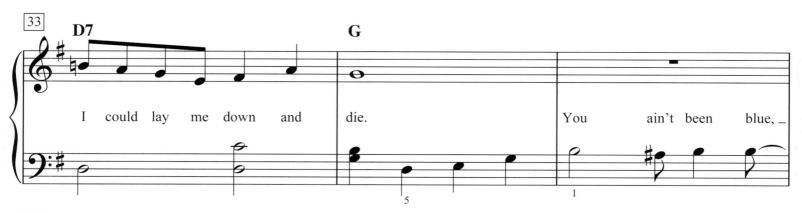

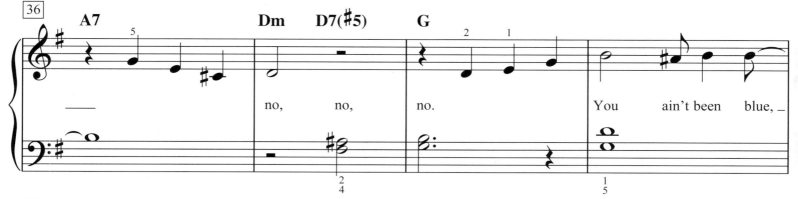

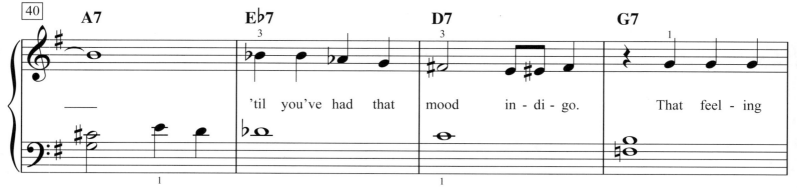

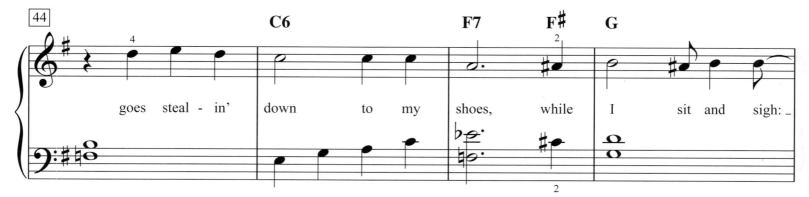

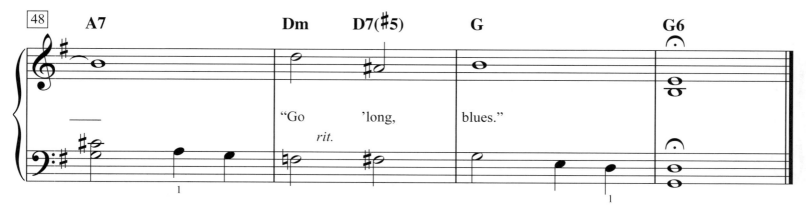

PERDIDO

Words by HARRY LENK and ERVIN DRAKE
Music by JUAN TIZOL
Arranged by Phillip Keveren

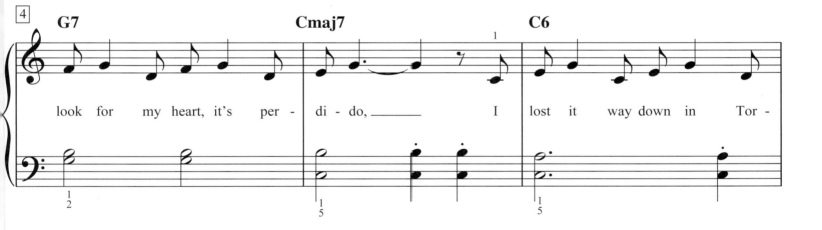

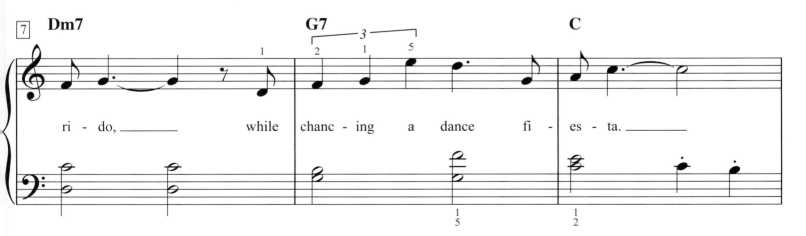

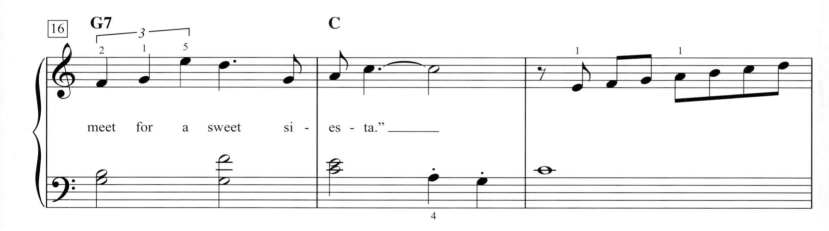

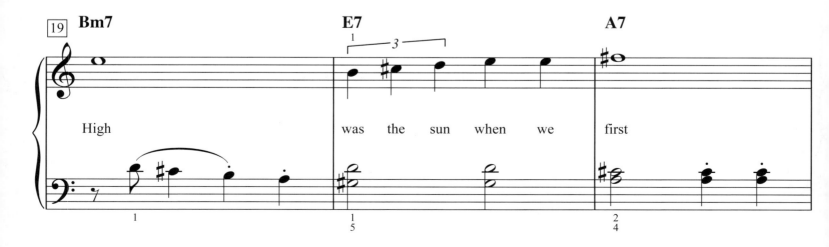

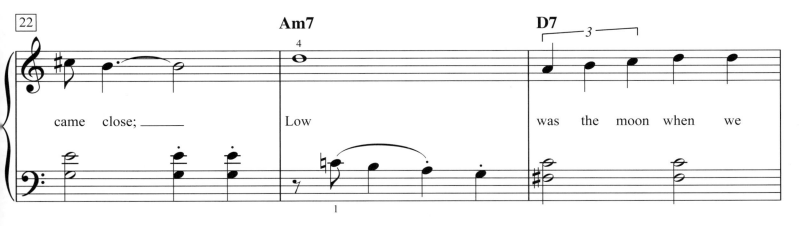

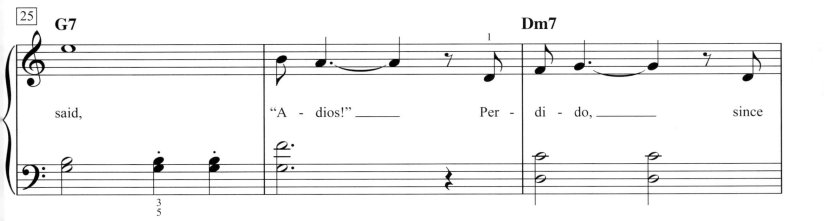

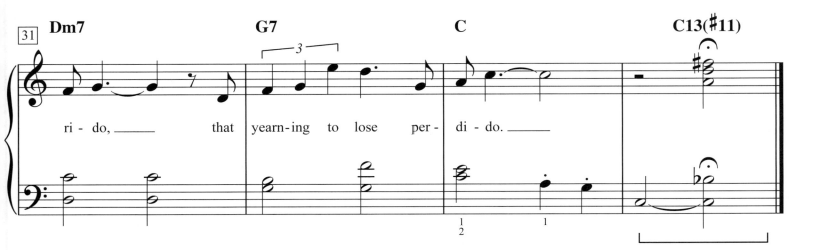

PRELUDE TO A KISS

Words by IRVING GORDON
and IRVING MILLS
Music by DUKE ELLINGTON
Arranged by Phillip Keveren

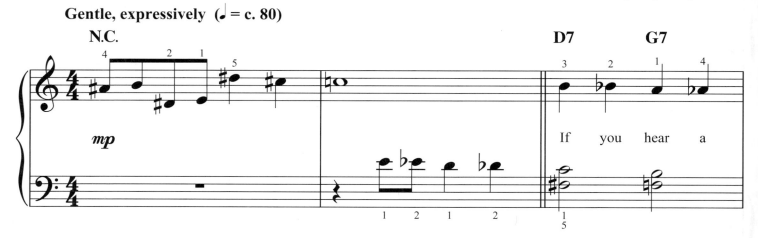

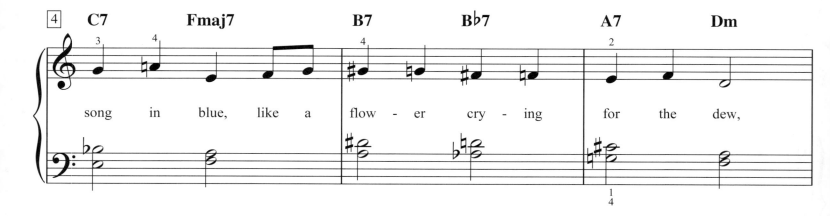

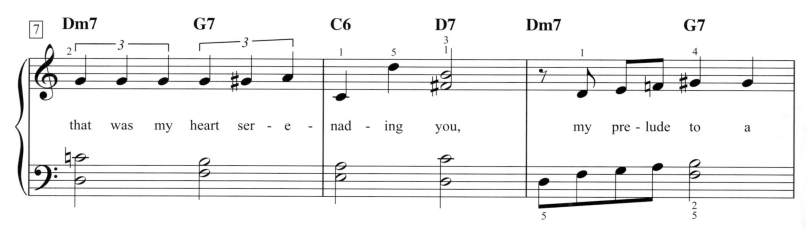

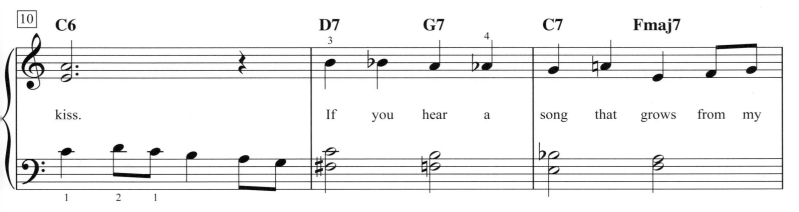

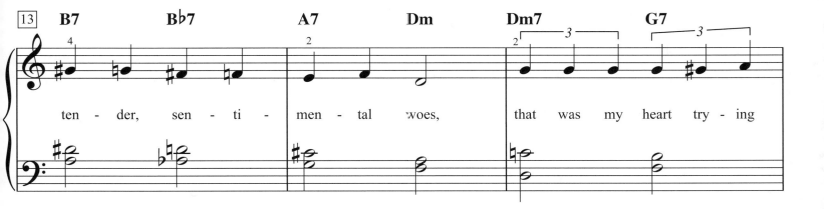

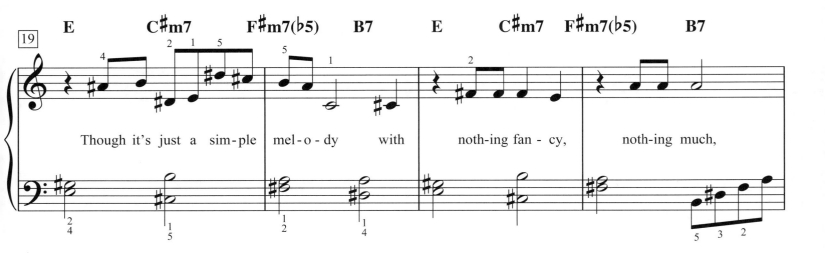

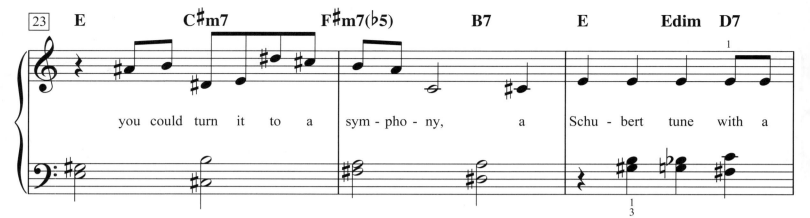

you could turn it to a sym-pho-ny, a Schu-bert tune with a

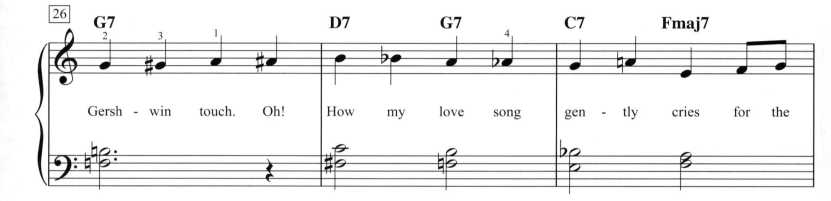

Gersh-win touch. Oh! How my love song gen-tly cries for the

ten-der-ness with-in your eyes. My love is a pre-lude that nev-er dies,

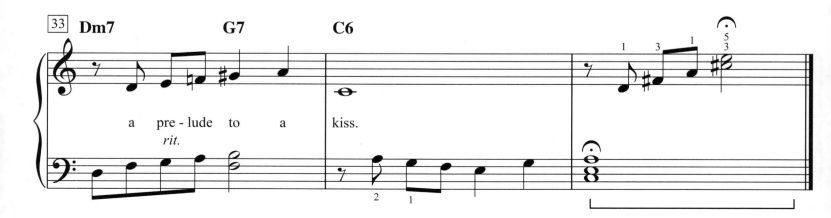

a pre-lude to a kiss.

SATIN DOLL
(Variations)

By DUKE ELLINGTON
Arranged by Phillip Keveren

Easy-going Swing (♩ = c. 120)

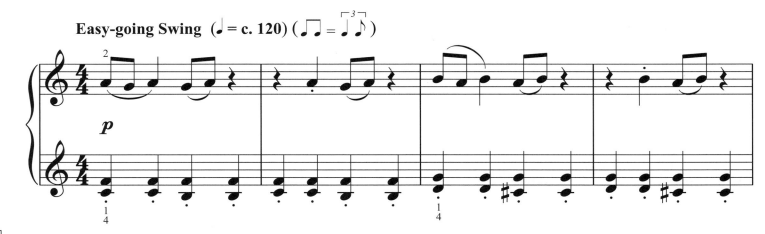

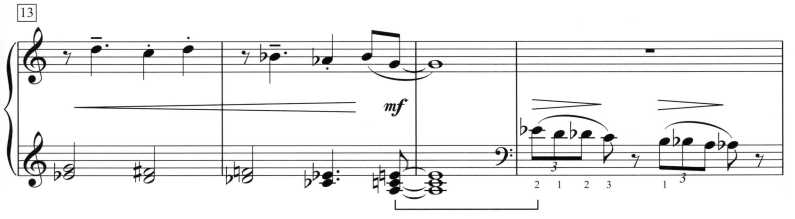

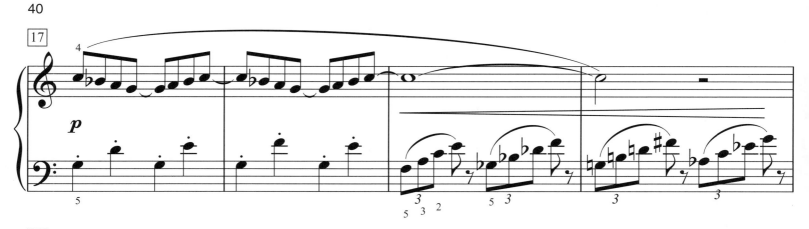

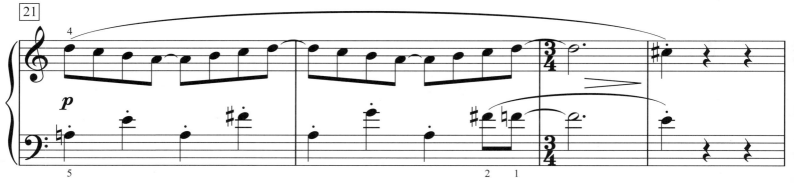

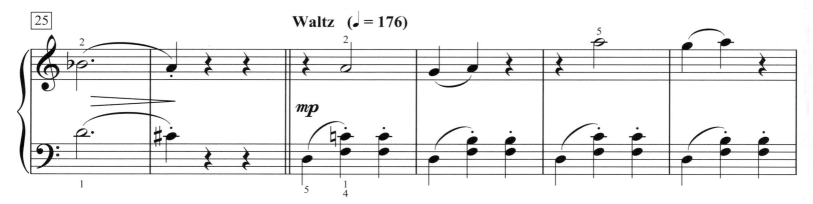

Waltz (♩ = 176)

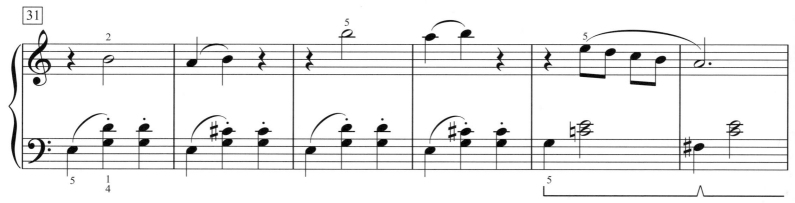

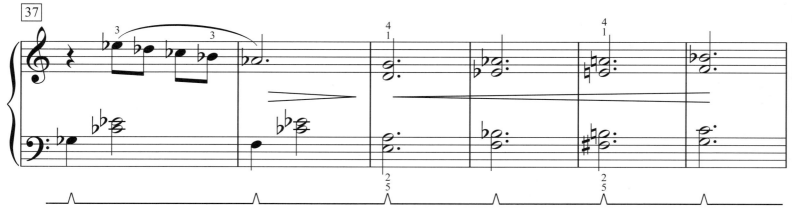

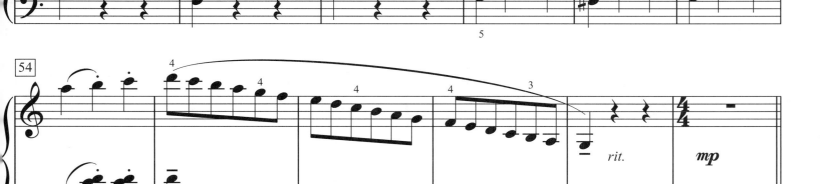

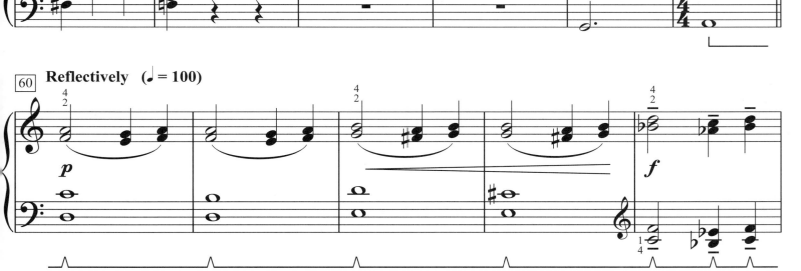

Reflectively (♩ = 100)

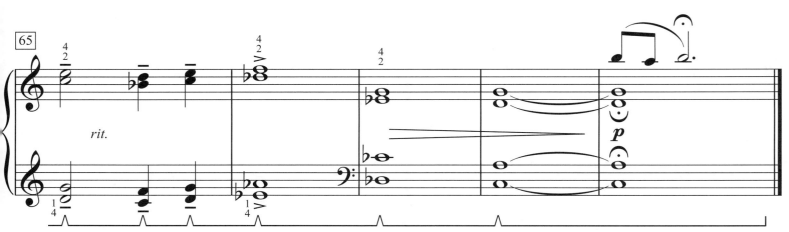

SOLITUDE

Words and Music by DUKE ELLINGTON,
EDDIE De LANGE and IRVING MILLS
Arranged by Phillip Keveren

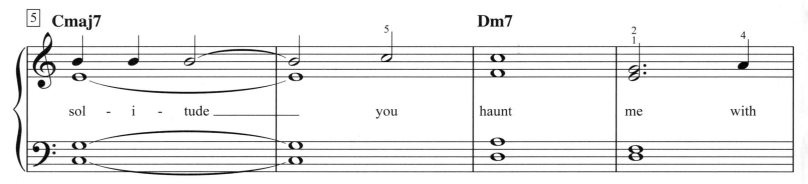

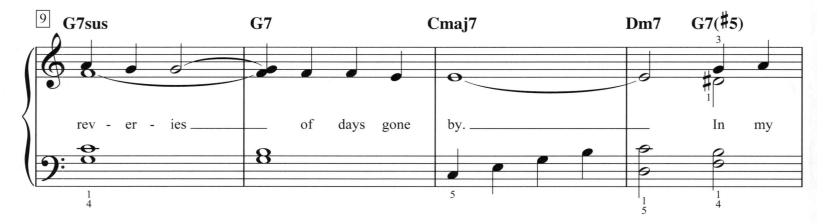

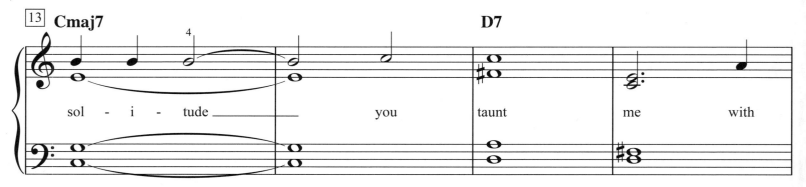

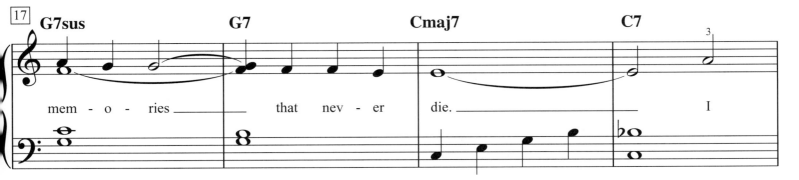

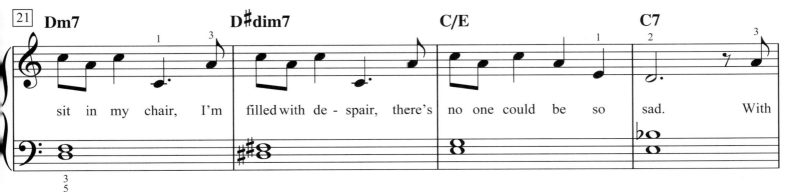

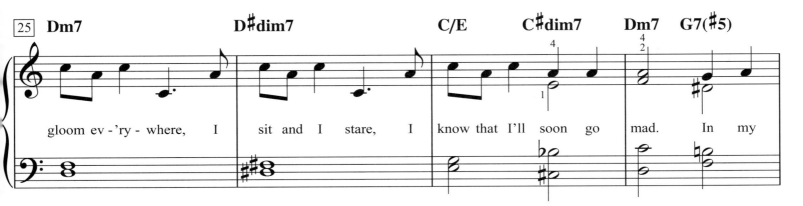

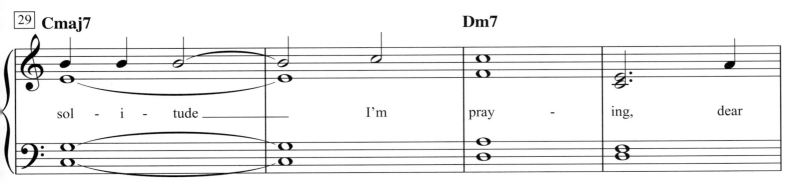

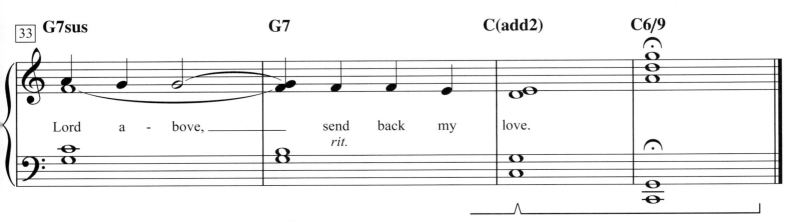

TAKE THE "A" TRAIN

Words and Music by BILLY STRAYHORN
Arranged by Phillip Keveren

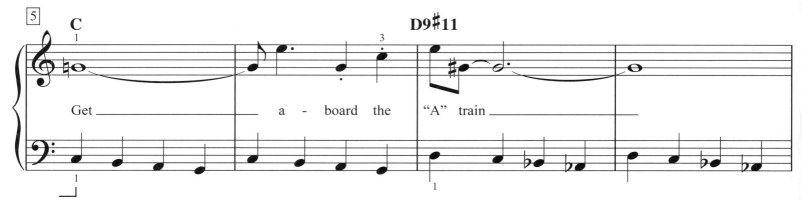

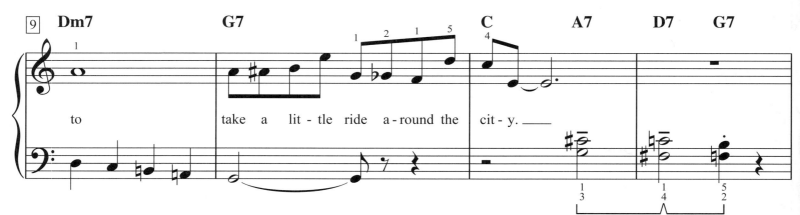

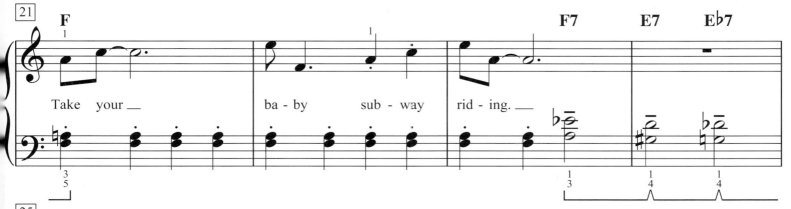

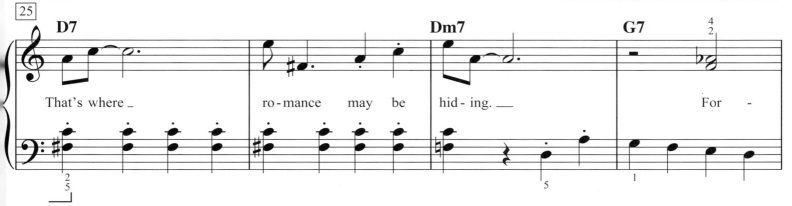

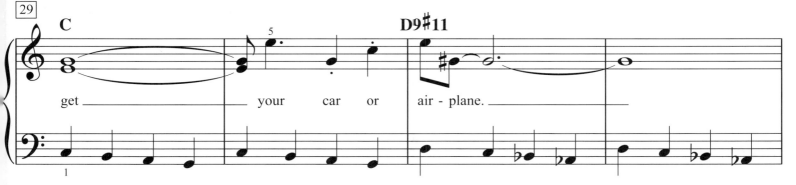

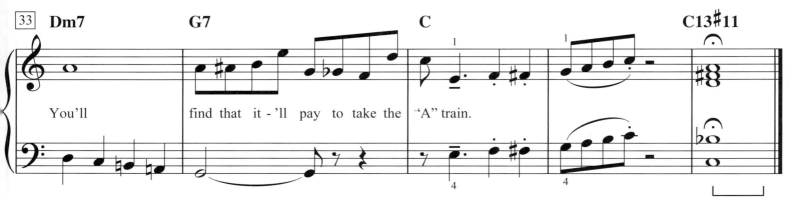

SOPHISTICATED LADY

Words and Music by DUKE ELLINGTON,
IRVING MILLS and MITCHELL PARISH
Arranged by Phillip Keveren

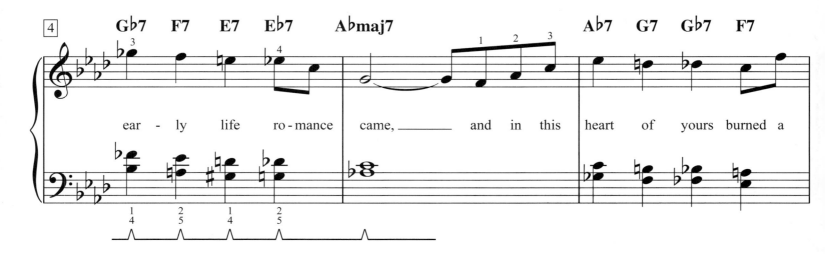

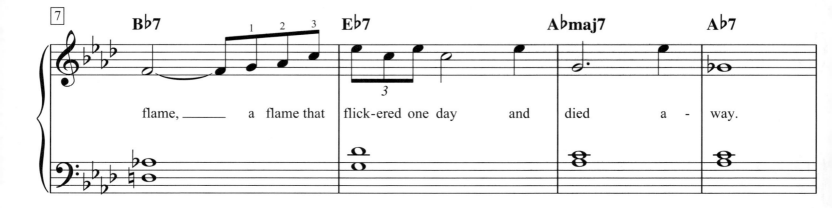

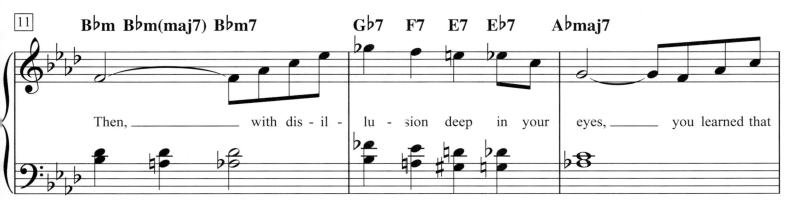

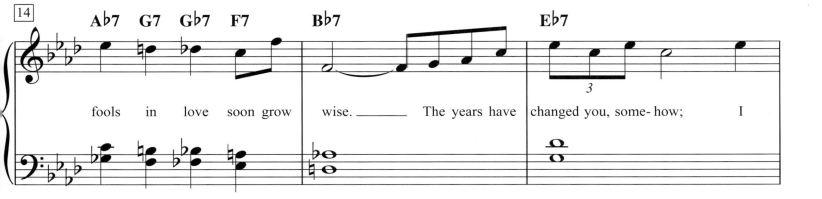

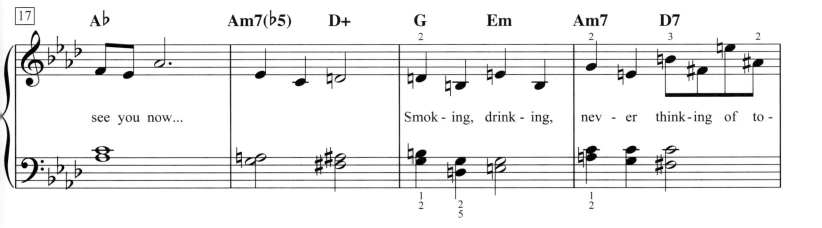

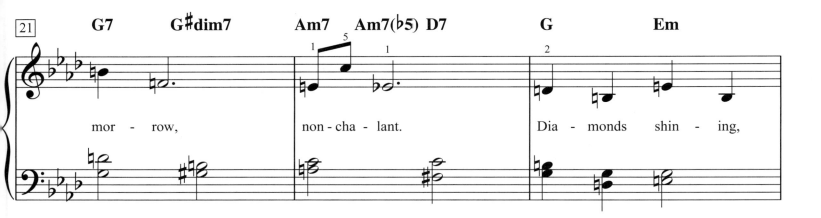

dancing, din-ing with some man in a res-tau-rant; is that all you real-ly want?

No,_____ so-phis-ti - cat - ed la-dy, I know,_____ you miss the

love you lost long a - go;_____ and when no-bod-y is nigh, you

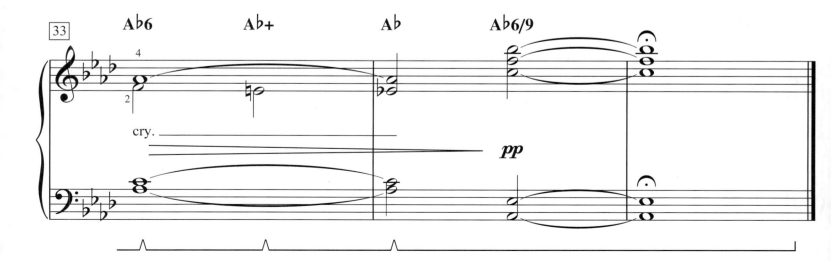

cry._____